When I first met Steve I was immediately aware
of his desire to cut through religion
genuine relationship with th
to become a tr
dent. Through
faced challenges
Godward. I recon
an open heart and   ...n by
the Holy Spirit int   ...ationship with
the Lord.

—JOHN CAIRNS
PRESIDENT, JOHN CAIRNS MINISTRIES
INTERNATIONAL TEAM LEADERS—
LEADERS NETWORK INTERNATIONAL

FROM
LEGAL
TO
Regal

FROM
LEGAL
TO
Regal

RELIGION *to* ROYALTY

STEVE HAWKINS

**CREATION
HOUSE**

FROM LEGAL TO REGAL by Steve Hawkins
Published by Creation House
A Charisma Media Company
600 Rinehart Road
Lake Mary, Florida 32746
www.charismamedia.com

Unless otherwise noted, all Scripture quotations are from the New American Standard Bible, Updated Edition. Copyright © 1960, 1962, 1963, 1968, 1971, 1972, 1973, 1975, 1977, 1995 by the Lockman Foundation. Used by permission. (www.Lockman.org)

Scripture quotations marked NIV are from the Holy Bible, New International Version of the Bible. Copyright © 1973, 1978, 1984, International Bible Society. Used by permission.

Design Director: Bill Johnson
Cover design by Terry Clifton

Library of Congress Cataloging-in-Publication Data: 2013946759
International Standard Book Number: 978-1-62136-683-6
E-book International Standard Book Number: 978-1-62136-684-3

While the author has made every effort to provide accurate telephone numbers and Internet addresses at the time of publication, neither the publisher nor the author assumes any responsibility for errors or for changes that occur after publication.

First edition

13 14 15 16 17 — 9 8 7 6 5 4 3 2 1
Printed in the United States of America

DEDICATION

From Legal to Regal is dedicated to you
who have held my hand in my journey
out of legalism into the Life of the Holy
Spirit. You know who you are. May many
more find His freedom!

Now the Lord is the Spirit, and where the Spirit
of the Lord is, there is liberty.

— 2 CORINTHIANS 3:17

CONTENTS

ACKNOWLEDGMENTS

THANKS TO CHARISMA House for their support and partnership.

Thanks to my family and friends who have so encouraged me in blessed times and bitter struggles.

New Zion Christian Fellowship in Welwyn Garden City, UK—you have embraced me in this genuine family—thank you. You have seen me at my best and worst.

Thank You, Jesus Christ—You are mine, and I am Yours.

INTRODUCTION

S UNDAY MORNING, IN church, the hymns and songs strike up, and we rejoice together, proclaiming the freedom that Jesus has bought us. Does this freedom seem more real on a Sunday morning?

It is for freedom that Christ has set us free.

—GALATIANS 5:1

Although He has bought our freedom and brings it into our experience through the Holy Spirit, where are we in terms of the vibrancy of our experience of it?

Freedom in Christ Jesus is a biblical truth that many welcome and seek to embrace. Is it fair to suggest that fewer of us live in a fulfilling reality of it?

More commonly, believers up and down the land live frustrated lives. There is a prevalent sense of struggle, striving, and failure among many. Disappointments have set in and taken up residence, clouding the view of spiritual realities. Prophetic promises appear to be parked on the shelf. The life of Christ lacks potency. The good news of the gospel seems to have taken on an ambiguity. Whilst the theology of what Jesus Christ did on the cross sits comfortably within our intellectual chamber, its reality seems to have left many of us untouched to a lesser or greater extent.

I suppose, in my own experience, I have been most aware of my own state when in the company of a freedom expressed in some of my fellow believers. The deficit has been evident.

It's not an exact science either, is it? We are all unique and have come to know His freedom to different degrees in various aspects of our lives. We do well not to compare ourselves with each other and, yet, we yearn for a more tangible experience with the life of Jesus.

In this book I would like to unpack some of the key realities that God has made available to each and every believer through the finished work of the cross. I am no theological expert. I hope and trust that what is written here will stand up to Scripture; clearly it can only be written from the revelation that I have had to date. For that, I trust the Holy Spirit, who has shown me, personally, what I would like to share—sometimes directly and, often, through the encouragement and ministry of others. Ultimately, as grateful as I am to those who have edified me and revealed much of what His freedom could be and has become to me, I choose to receive it all from Him, the ultimate Revelator and owner of the most generous hands—His own!

I have no idea, really, how to write a book. This is my first. So, dear guinea pigs, welcome to my sandpit and enjoy my fumbling attempt to put together something

that I hope will encourage you and speak into your life!
I am learning not to take myself too seriously, to enjoy
the river of His grace, and to live the Life He has so
amazingly purchased and given to each of us in Jesus.

We really are, all, so precious to Him.

From time to time you will see a line or two set in
italics. These are usually short prayers that you might
like to join me in.

A generous, happy God wants to hang out with you,
build you up, teach you personally, and show you who
you really are in Him. If anything in the following
pages comes as fresh and a surprise to you, I honestly
hope that you enjoy it and embrace Him in it, shifting
into a new reality of the life of Christ: Christ, the hope
of glory in you.

Chapter 1

BEGINNINGS

*God has chosen you from the beginning
for salvation through sanctification by
the Spirit and faith in the truth.*

—2 THESSALONIANS 2:13

I HAD ONE OF those fairly dramatic conversions. Well, it was to me. Brought up in a Christian, church-going home, I didn't really first meet with God until I was at university in Birmingham in the UK.

There were stirrings before that, mind you. A theme that I will probably return to frequently is that of God's surpassing and mind-dazzling knowledge of each of us, who were known and called in Christ before the foundation of the world (Eph. 1:4). Just think on that for a moment. We all, who have come into relationship with God, through Jesus Christ, share that in common. *Before the foundation of the world* is a long time before any of us had an inkling of what had occurred in heavenly places. It's almost incredible, but not so, because it is true, so we do well to believe it and to ask God to show us the reality of it. And that He is delighted to do. We really must have been worth it for Him to make such an investment in us.

As a young teen I began to desire to visit my local parish church for the early Sunday morning service. For a season, I felt guilty if I didn't do so, and while I have since discovered that much of that initial motivation was really an expression of inner guilt and turbulence and of a need to belong, it nevertheless began to move me towards Jesus. I was, to whatever degree it might have been, taking intentional steps towards Him. He, of course, had taken the initiative to draw me in His love, but, believe me, I was a long, long way from knowing any of this at the time.

I wonder how many regular churchgoers attend from similar motivations, week after week. God knows each of them and longs to fill the substitute ritual with a real relationship.

In my later teens, after gaining a place at university in Birmingham, God drew near again. I began attending meetings at the Christian Union and saw that many of those guys and gals had something I didn't have. It was something personal. Their eyes were alive and a solidity seemed to underpin their outlook, a genuine cheerfulness bubbled within, and I knew I didn't have that. You know when you don't have the real thing, and you know when you see the evidence of it in others.

Some people try to explain, with many words, how amazing their experience of Jesus is. As wonderful as that is, I confess that I prefer to just "see" Him and the evidence of His presence in others. That speaks volumes to me.

There is something rather sad about someone who belongs to a church and clings desperately to that sense of corporate identity, yet knowing in their heart of hearts that there is a sizeable credibility gap between what they profess and what they live. Oh, we can all be there on occasions; I certainly can be and have no desire to point a finger. Maybe, more seriously, for a minority, the weekly church involvement is a well-practiced performance, even a sham. And it could so easily be remedied were the masks to drop!

Lord, let our church environments be real so that You are welcome to touch us in our deepest hearts. Let the effort of keeping up appearances dissipate so that Your Holy Spirit is released to meet us. Amen.

I don't know exactly when I first invited Jesus to be my Lord and Savior; it could have happened on a number of public occasions and countless private ones. But I do remember when the Holy Spirit first kissed my face, and in so doing, knocked me to the floor.

There was a Jesus Heals crusade in Birmingham, UK, with international evangelist Steve Ryder. After a lively charismatic service which included a time of very free praise and worship, he ministered to various people at the end of the meeting (I tend to think of services as meetings rather than services—the latter term reminds me of the more "churchy" experiences of my earlier youth) and finally invited those who would like to feel a touch from God to come to the front.

The meeting had been an eye opener to me. The genuine freedom and exuberance around me was something I didn't have. I remember trying to dance (because other people were), and my feet felt like lead. Whatever or whoever was inspiring them was not yet a reality to me in this way.

As I began to make my way to the front, I became aware that I was finding it hard to move. My steps were labored, and I felt slightly drunk; the atmosphere around me was thick with the presence of God. I knew it was the presence of God. I could feel Him. I kept walking forward and arrived at the altar to join a long line of others across it that had come, like me, to receive a holy touch.

I remember Steve Ryder explaining that God was going to touch us, that he (Steve) would lightly touch us on our forehead. That would be the only physical touch from him.

He began ministering along the line. I remember waiting for that touch on my forehead; when it came—bam—the next thing I knew, I was lying on the floor. There was nothing contrived or forced about that! God had personally touched me and literally swept me off my feet.

I had no idea then, of course, that this is one of the characteristics of our amazing, loving and, (I will say even as a bloke!) romantic God. He loves to love us; He loves to sweep us off our feet in a multitude of ways. If ever an earthly bride wanted to be swept off her feet, so shall the bride of Christ be!

This might sound a bit odd to men who are looking for the reality of God. Being swept off your feet sounds rather girlie, doesn't it? If so, think of it more as a solid impact upon your heart. Power and love wrapped up in one, an affirmation that we men were built for and long to know in the core of our being.

This experience in Birmingham birthed a fire in me. The baptism in the Holy Spirit (as I later learned it to have been) launched a fervor for Jesus in my life. But the road to come was not going to be a smooth one.

Chapter 2

ROCKY ROAD

*It is not those who are healthy who need
a physician, but those who are sick.*

—Matthew 9:12

T HE FIRE WAS undeniable, this passion that I had for Him. I was "sold out" as you may say. But I was also (unknowingly) very broken and, at the time, had no inkling of the flawed person, the flawed self, that this wonderful Holy Spirit had come to make His home in.

The Holy Spirit had certainly taken up residence in my life and made me His own. But there was going to be a lot of fixing to do. I had become a new creation in Christ, but my old nature, the one that I had lived with and through for the last twenty or so years, was in chaos. Of course, the truth was that old me had been crucified at the cross and was now dead, but I was a long way from reckoning it, I simply did not have the understanding or revelation of this. I had been hurt in my former years to no small degree, especially through bullying at school. Some of it in today's terms of reference would have amounted to abuse.

I was an on-fire believer, but a harsh, judgmental one, and one who assumed that all on-fire believers should probably be like me! If they weren't, then they probably were not on fire enough. My zeal inspired some of those around me in the Christian Union, but as real as that was, I had deep seated issues that I did not yet even know of, let alone heard the Lord speak to me about.

You see, I had become redeemed, as a whole, but much of my life was, as yet, untouched by God's love and grace. I was broken and insecure.

SCHOOL

Prior to my move to Birmingham, I had gone to an excellent grammar school in Essex, England. We worked hard, were pushed to excel, and our teachers used their expertise to work with us to ensure that we maximized our potential.

I would later understand that much of my self-worth was going to become wrapped up in success and performance. I was going to become a champion striver, and that is neither a title nor lifestyle that I would wish upon anyone!

I have seen a lot of striving in the body of Christ. God

sees our hearts, but there is a better way. The flow of His life in and through us will negate the need to strive. His enabling is sufficient to accomplish the business that He is about. Some people strive in a bid to make a project work that God has not involved Himself with. Others strive for attention and affirmation when the Holy Spirit would bring healing and wholeness to them. He wants us to know that He has already accepted us and brought us near (Eph. 2:13).

I had pretty much always known that I wanted to go to university. My teachers skillfully worked with me to give me the best opportunity, one which (by God's unseen grace) I took. It was also here, at school, that I studied music to an advanced level and first became acquainted with the skill of improvising music. Oh, I wasn't doing the improvising myself; that was superbly demonstrated by a couple of classmates who would glee-fully rattle off 12-bar blues and jazz-inspired refrains—boy, I was hooked! I still love that kind of music! What I didn't know at the time was that even then God was planting in me the seeds of a desire and an ability to do the same. Now, many years later, I freely improvise on keyboards as I enjoy leading prophetic worship in dif-ferent styles and seek to reproduce the sounds of heaven right here. It's such fun. The anointing is precious. God's blessings make us rich, and He adds no sorrow to them (Prov. 10:22)!

The presence of God is going to come in such anointing among us that people will receive His ministry without a hand being laid on them. They will hear from Him, receive His counsel and comfort, and receive physical healing. This is on the way and has already started to happen. The blessings of God enrich, empower and restore. His presence is worth more than the best laid out program if that program reduces the Holy Spirit to a spectator.

Recently, a lady from my fellowship shared with me that God had released her into a new freedom during our time of worship together. The words of the song had become flesh to her and worked themselves in her as she worshipped. Wonderful Holy Spirit! It's great to sing a song when our singing of it accompanies the Holy Spirit's activation of what is being sung.

The song's proclamation of freedom in the presence of the Lord is based on the scripture:

> Now the Lord is the Spirit, and where the Spirit
> of the Lord is, there is liberty.
> —2 CORINTHIANS 3:17

Does freedom reign? Does He reign here? Is freedom being activated amongst those who are worshipping?

By the way, I love that verse. It's a great one to show anyone who suggests that the Holy Spirit is simply an anonymous power rather than a person. The verse shows us that the Holy Spirit is Lord, as Jesus is Lord!

The downside of my school experience was, as I have alluded to, that I was quite severely bullied throughout my time there. I came to realize, a long time later, that this had been a satanic assignment against my prophetic calling. If there is one quality that a prophetic outlook requires, it is boldness in the speaker. The bullying agenda against me had been designed to make me timid. At the time, I had no idea of the unseen battle arrayed against me. I was thoroughly intimidated and, I suppose, quite afraid through much of my time at school. I did not appreciate, at the time, the sense of isolation and mistrust that the enemy was seeking to plant within me. The insecurity, especially throughout my developing teenage years (which have enough natural challenges of their own), stayed with me and also protected a deep-seated anger. I was angry that I was apparently so vulnerable to attack, despite authority figures being aware of it.

I also had no idea of how controlling this bullying behavior was and of how controlling I was going to become as a result of it. The need to control was born from an inner sense of desperation. Who was going to protect me if I didn't maneuver and do my utmost to avoid the abuse that seemed to have almost free access to me?

We really need to have our eyes opened in the body of Christ to see that controlling behavior is nothing less than witchcraft. Even well-meaning, controlling behavior (and some of that can come from Christians) births from the same pot. We need to address this squarely in the face, as it is not a minor issue within the Church. Whenever we seek to impose our will over that of someone else concerning their life, we are operating in controlling behavior and actually partnering with witchcraft. If this sounds over the top, I am nevertheless convinced it is true. We have no right to try to make of someone anything other than what the Holy Spirit is working in them. When we encourage and pray for others (and let's certainly do that), whose will are we seeking to enforce?

Alongside my endeavors at university, I joined a church in my locality at home, in Hertfordshire. The flavor of this church was very similar to what I had come to experience in Birmingham—except more so! I was in a charismatic, bubbling environment, one in which the Word of God was fully embraced. Thank you, Lord, that you planted me there.

PLANTING

The Holy Spirit calls us to be a part of the body of Christ. He expresses Jesus to the world through the church. He would have us planted in a church family where we can grow, be nurtured, nurture others and learn to assume kingdom responsibilities. We mature in a myriad of ways as we rub shoulders with our brothers and sisters and allow the grace of God to move in the midst.

No church body will be perfect. Certainly not if you or I become part of it!

My newfound environment was a good start to my life in Christ.

Chapter 3

GROWING UP IN FAITH

The place where they had gathered together was shaken.

—ACTS 4:31

THIS CHURCH REALLY was a hot house! The presence of the Lord among us was, at times, awesome. I mean awesome in its original sense because today everything from an ice cream to a goal scored in football to an exceptional cup of coffee to an action movie is routinely described as awesome. God decided that this apparently insignificant little church (I use the term *insignificant* respectfully) was hugely significant in His eyes, and that He liked spending time with us. I remember on one occasion looking at a map; the church building was not even marked on it!

The leaders graciously embraced me, and, as body

ministry was a given there, opportunities to minister came early and frequently. I have to honor the approach of the leaders who sought to encourage the moving of the Holy Spirit and allowed many in the body to have a go when it came to expressing Jesus in various ways. Most meetings were very open; usually there was an extended time of worship to begin with, but not always. Proceedings were punctuated with prophetic words, the sharing of Bible verses, pictures, impressions, and prayer for physical and emotional healing. Prayer for deliverance happened on occasions too. Sometimes we would pray into these revelations, seizing the moment, seeking to flow with the Holy Spirit as He revealed needs and His wishes among us. People worshiped in their seats, on their feet, on their faces and in dance. Much of the ministry came through church members, but on occasions we welcomed a range of visiting ministries of different flavors and styles! The key was that the leaders sought out those who they believed God wanted to use to invest in us as a body (spiritually I mean). Whoever shared, we were looking for the "now" word in the church and for the move of God.

I began to cut my teeth in worship on the keyboard in the church. I had already become aware that God was anointing my fingers and producing healing music through them. A prophetic word I had received previously had indicated that this was going to happen. I began to get involved with leading worship and found that I didn't want to try to read the music in front of me. I couldn't do it. Rather, I played freely and the congregation sang over me. At times, we did not play songs at all. I just played the piano or keyboard and the presence of God would come with His agenda. There were many varied agendas: healing, warfare, and breakthrough. Sometimes I found myself playing very gently and at other times quite militantly. It was an expression of God's voice in my fingers. I still enjoy this line of ministry today, and it has deepened considerably since these early days. It has also become much easier as I have learned to flow with Him and not strive in my own mind.

He has much to show us about the heavenly realms. They are closer than we imagine. Ephesians 2 states that we actually live there, but many of us have not quite grasped the reality of that yet. How do you think He wants to express Himself through you? Some good questions to ask ourselves are, *What do I enjoy doing?* and, *What would I like to do?* These can be useful indicators as to what is on our hearts.

This life of Christ we are coming to consider is for all of us in Jesus. In fact, we are sometimes impressed by those who appear a little super-spiritual, but His life is not super-spiritual. It is very powerful in itself and does not need any padding from us.

I also began to share openly in the church as opportunities arose and were presented to me. The Lord frequently gave me passages from the Bible to speak from and our open style of meetings enabled me and many others to grow in this environment of collective encouragement. I preached on some Sunday mornings and was encouraged, again, to be open to prophetic ministry as part of this. Little did I appreciate at the time that this prophetic emphasis would grow into a more significant calling on my life. I loved to share in the flow of the Spirit—I loved (and still do love) the spontaneity. I knew I was not sharing from my own inspiration or learning, but from Him.

On the not so positive side, I was quite driven. Enthusiasm is a good quality; being driven is not so healthy. I struggled to make and maintain relationships on many levels. I was not living from a place of rest (more on that a little later). I believe that my insecurities also contributed to this sense of being driven. I wanted to be accepted; I felt I had to work hard at belonging, although I did belong. I was unsure, at times, in terms of what commitment looked like. It was a potent mix of a very Spirit-filled environment coupled with, perhaps, an element of fear that one might miss what God wanted to do. Insecurity, fear, and a need to achieve do not make for a healthy mixture.

Mixture is probably a good term for this, and I have pondered on it from time to time. There can be a strong anointing in a church, but at the same time our busyness coupled with elements of legalism can take us out of the divine rest He has purchased for us, even in so-called charismatic circles. I have since learned that this is not unusual. God is very gracious and loves to express Himself as He is permitted to. But there can be a tendency in us to try to make church work when, actually, we probably need to yield and let Him do the molding and building.

The more plates we try to spin and keep spinning, the harder it is to stay at the pace of the Spirit. God can operate His own plates; our part is to live from rest in Him (more on this later) and allow Him to be the senior partner.

I continued to grow in the gifts of the Spirit, ministering frequently, running a house group and later joining the leadership team—all fine and dandy, and certainly busy. But all was not well within.

This came to light in a major way when I went to Toronto Airport Christian Fellowship in 2003!

Chapter 4

TORONTO AIRPORT CHRISTIAN FELLOWSHIP

Take My yoke upon you and learn from Me,
for I am gentle... YOU WILL FIND REST... For
My yoke is easy and My burden is light.

—MATTHEW 11:29–30

THE PEOPLE AT Toronto Airport Christian Fellowship (TACF) were marvelous. From the moment we arrived, we were encouraged to drop our baggage, our labels, and our responsibilities. I was Steve. *That's it.* Not Steve with whatever I did at work, not Steve the worship leader; I was just Steve. It wasn't going to be a comfortable ride, however.

I have to be honest: the whole Father heart thing— it didn't come easily to me. Not that I had had an unhealthy relationship with my earthly dad, but TACF was where I was going to discover something new about the Father's love. During my five weeks in Toronto at the Leaders School of Ministry, I cried a lot, shouted a lot, and shared a lot. I wrestled hard with the notion that, well, I was all right, that God liked me, and that I didn't need to do anything at all to maintain his attention and affection. This was not easy for someone as driven as I was to receive. Inside I had been crying out to know this, but, to a degree, the cry had been suffocated with a lot of activity and, yes, ministry. I had very serious doubts that He really accepted me and even, at times, that I belonged to Him.

From time to time I had experienced a deep sense of fear, guilt, and unease. Usually this occurred when I was in a meeting and an altar call was made. I came to dread such occasions as I felt compelled (I will return to this theme of compulsion later) to respond and make sure that I was saved.

At one meeting at TACF, during a conference (The Party Is Here) I was attending with most of the other delegates from the School of Ministry, just as the message was drawing to a close, the speaker invited those who would like ministry to come forward. I hoped that there would not be an altar call; I was dreading that niggling sense of *you really need to go up, to show you are committed.* To my horror, the speaker first said he was going to give an opportunity for those who either didn't know the Lord or who felt that they wanted to recommit to Him. This was like a red rag to a bull. I was in a raw, vulnerable state, my emotional wound oozing as I sat there. I felt the dread. I felt I had to obey. This was not, of course, the Comforter prompting me, but in my bondage the Holy Spirit was allowing me to see the extent of it.

This was not an expression of the abundant life of Christ. The Holy Spirit never moves us by using fear. There is no fear in God. There is no fear in love. As the Scripture says:

> The one who fears is not perfected in love.
>
> —1 JOHN 4:18

Wearing my leader's badge (oh, Lord, the embarrassment) I went up to the front.

I was the only one. In a hall of about two thousand people.

I still cringe as I remember this. God was wonderfully gracious, as was the minister, who laid his hand on me, looked at me and said with discernment, "You've done this before, haven't you?"

I acknowledged that I had, He prayed a blessing on me, and that was it. I felt relief that I had been obedient (to my mind), but the truth was that my compliance with the lie that I had needed to respond to the altar call in the first place only served to strengthen it. I would later learn that I would need to disarm these accusations by refusing to respond to them, thereby silencing them.

The point I am trying to highlight here is that I did not know *God's nature.* I was an experienced worship leader, house group leader, had been on missions, and was experienced in the prophetic and in preaching. But inside I was, frankly, a mess. Where was the abundant life Jesus had promised me and bought for me?

I, as you are if you belong to Christ, was a royal son of the King of kings but I was enslaved to fear. Does this sound to you like a healthy lifestyle lived from heavenly places?

There in Toronto, God was showing me that I—Steve—*just me*—mattered to Him, and that He loved me enough to strip away all the responsibilities and expectations (mine and those of others) and provide a space, a window of opportunity, for me to come out of unreality and into a place of wholeness. To reference the slogan of a popular cosmetics company, I was worth it. Real ministry was, in the future, going to be built from a different place from where I had been, one of acceptance and rest. But, boy, these were very early days for that revelation!

It's so easy to become what, and live as, others expect you to. The price is high. God is jealous for us to fulfill our unique potential. Parents reading this will hopefully concur that a good parent wants to see each child blossom in their own, unique fashion. I wonder where that desire springs from!

Even when we discover our brokenness, as Graham Cooke says, God is never disillusioned with us because He never had any illusions about us in the first place!

People are sometimes disappointed with us because they have appointed us to certain roles, behaviors, or molds which we decide or realize are not ours. The appointment therefore becomes a *dis*-appointment as we refuse to co-operate. This disengagement is crucial so that we can live as we were designed to and be fulfilled in who God created us to be, rather than to satisfy the expectations of others.

This is a foundation to us living in freedom in Christ and enjoying a supernatural walk with Him, unfettered.

MOVING

Now while I was at TACF, the Lord told me directly that He was moving me out of the church where I had been for twenty years! This was not expected, and yet, when I heard this, it was as if I had known it for some time.

It's important to test prophetic words. I have learned not to receive (to own, to take on) words which do not resonate with me. On this occasion it resonated clearly and deeply.

We really are supernatural creatures! God also, through the ministry of Ivan and Isabel Allum, revealed much to me about my destiny and calling in God. Honestly, it blew my socks off! I had been familiar with the prophetic but this was detail extraordinaire. And wonderful. And gloriously impossible in natural terms. Only God would be able to bring this calling to fruition, and I delighted in that and still do so. I saw that God had invested in me and was committed to His investment. I was beginning to see something new of His heart for me.

And He has the same heart for you. Living as a son

of the kingdom requires knowing beyond all reasoning that God's heart is generous and good towards us *all the time*. His nature is to be that way; it does not depend on how well we think we are doing.

He does not lay burdens on us. We live in Him—*you and I live in Him*—and He builds us, and thereby builds His church. What an amazing perspective that is, that in each and every way He builds something of the kingdom (which is indestructible and eternal) in each and every one us, and the whole Church is strengthened!

At TACF I was able to get a glimpse of why I had experienced such pressures and challenges in my life to this point. He was building me for what was coming! But the messy times were far from over.

Chapter 5

NEW PASTURES

The lines have fallen to me in pleasant places;
Indeed, my heritage is beautiful to me.

—Psalm 16:6

U PON RETURNING TO the UK, I left my church
through a gradual process that took about two
years. It's one thing to have the word of the
Lord, but sometimes the outworking of that is not as we
expect, and we need to continue to walk with Him so
that He does things His way.

How gracious He is.

I remember on one occasion I was feeling rather
impatient. I went out for a walk and said to the Lord,
Right, I have had Your word; I am going to leave the
church now. When I got home from the walk, an email

from one of the other TACF delegates was waiting for me, warning me that the Lord had shown them that I was about to step into a pit! God knew that He had a better way. He was going to lead me out of one church and into another.

It's a big deal to move from a church that you have been part of for a considerable period of time. It's important to hear from God and to know that He is behind the move. He plants us, and, I believe, He uproots us to re-pot us somewhere for the next stage of our development, and, who knows, for the next seasons in what God is doing both in the church family we are leaving, and the one we are joining.

God graciously gave me a further prophetic confirmation concerning moving on from the church, and the leaders came to a unanimous consensus that God was doing this. The Lord also gave me a dream that I would leave the church in unity and joy—and that is precisely how it happened.

Thank God for His supernatural gifts and ways of speaking to us!

I had a dream. In the dream I was walking arm in arm with a girl. The presence of God fell on us, and we were laughing. I knew that the girl represented the church I was leaving, and that He was going to ensure that He led me out in His perfect order, in joy and in right relationship. Praise God!

At my final meeting there, there was singing and dancing and people generously affirmed me, my ministry among them, and that to come. In fact, the meeting was hijacked! You might be thinking that they sang and danced because they wanted me to leave—I will pray for your discernment!

DREAMS

I will add here that dreams have played a key role in my walk with the Lord. I would encourage you to ask Him to speak to you in dreams. Commit to Him that realm; it is an important one. You are probably going to go to sleep just about every night of your life, so that's a lot of time for Him to minister to you. He is awake, after all, and so is your spirit-man. Dreams are a wonderful resource; you will see the Old Testament and New Testament are full of them! I have had reassuring dreams from the Lord, warnings, and dreams that put perspective on what I have been walking through at that time.

Once, I was in an emotional mess, and I had a dream. I dreamed that I was walking through a deep forest. I then saw, from above, a man walking parallel to me alongside the forest. I knew that God was showing me that Jesus was alongside me in my difficulty and confusion, in a place where I couldn't see the wood from the trees.

If you had nightmares as a child or have had them up to this point in your life, if the dream realm has been one of fear for you, you can shut that door right now. God does not want you to be robbed in this valuable arena of your life. You can pray now:

Lord Jesus, I cancel and erase any enemy agenda in my dream realm in Jesus' name. Re-ignite my dream realm, Lord, for Your kingdom. Reveal to me anything You want to about my life and about kingdom life in my dreams. I am open to You, Lord, and listening. You are good in all You do, and there is no fear in Your love. Amen.

Yes, amen!

The Lord led me to a wonderful church which I am part of today. Let me tell you more about what has happened since.

TRANSITION

The Lord showed me that I was joining this church as a transition in my life. Well, six years later, I am still there and learning about what transition can involve! We may assume that a transition is brief; but, as the saying goes, "It ain't necessarily so."

In essence, the transition has been a continuation and development of what (I perceive to have) started in Toronto. We sometimes think of a transition as a "between place." It is that, but we may not appreciate that the transition itself is a rich, key process of God working in our lives. I thought of transition as a temporary stop. *I wonder where I'm going next* I thought. This was a misunderstanding, premature, and only part of the picture. Irrespective of where I may live physically, the real work has been an internal, kingdom work, not merely a geographical one.

It has been geographical in that I have now moved to Welwyn Garden City in Hertfordshire, UK to live among my church people. But that has been a secondary factor to key internal changes in my heart.

The real transition has been internal, and it is the internal changes that truly change us externally. Time shows us that, doesn't it? Have you ever thought that you desperately needed a holiday or a change of scene (and there is nothing wrong at all with those), but on returning home nothing has really changed or moved on?

There are moments when God touches us, when He brings a shift in our lives, and the repercussions are huge. Whatever the vessel he uses to do this, He has wrought something in you. Maybe you walked through a challenging circumstance, perhaps you read a book and caught a revelation of God's nature or of something heavenly, perhaps a simple word or piece of advice (or correction) from someone touched you deeply and opened a way ahead for you.

In *The Christian's Secret to a Happy Life*, Hannah Whitehall Smith expresses beautifully the ways in which God uses many "second causes" in our lives, some of them pleasant and some otherwise, but that ultimately we can consider Him as the "first cause." This does not mean that He has instigated all that we live through, but we could say that He has rubber stamped it as purposeful in His economy.

Lord, You see each of us, millions and millions of us, and somehow You manage (with ease) to track each of us and our progress;

29

You intervene in our lives and make plans for us, in You, and You reveal more and more of Yourself to us. You actually live inside us and want to increasingly live through us. Live Your Life in us! Thank You, Lord.

We died on the cross with Him. We died! We are dead and now alive in Christ. It could be fairly simple, but how we have complicated it! Sometimes others, as bound as we have been, have contributed to that complicating agenda, and sometimes it has been our own brokenness and blindness that have been major factors.

With the encouragement of my leaders, and as part of this body, I have begun to see that all that God requires of me is to be Steve, and to allow Him to reveal His love to me. A natural consequence of this is that more of His love is seen in and through me. Likewise for you too! This is a major step along the path of beginning to live His life—the life of a royal son, a regal life.

There is much to do in the kingdom of God. But it is important to remember that we are, first of all, human beings and not human doings. And there is quite a lot that needs to be *un-done* in many of us.

Let's have a little look at that.

Chapter 6

KNOTS AND TANGLES

*Water encompassed me to the point of
death. The great deep engulfed me, Weeds
were wrapped around my head.*

—JONAH 2:5

AVE YOU EVER ordered a product through a catalogue or online and excitedly anticipated the arrival of the box? It is delivered; you rather uneasily open it, having heard a somewhat suspicious tinkling and shifting of the contents within. Disappointed, you realize that the product has been damaged in transit. You have a box of damaged goods.

Without any wish at all to inspire thoughts of self-pity, damage has occurred in our lives, to a greater or lesser degree. The deep has engulfed us, and weeds may have almost suffocated our hope.

We are all in transit! The Bible says that we are aliens on earth. We were born from heaven, have been seated in heaven with Jesus, and one day we will live there transparently and perfectly. If we really could see this as the reality that it is, our perspective on many aspects of our lives would change radically.

I hesitate to say that we are all damaged goods, but I can't help it. We *are* all damaged goods. Or, we *were*. Our restoration has been paid for, and, more than that, a new creation has replaced the old one.

However you may feel, a new creation has replaced the old one.

We once lived for years under a covenant of darkness, away from intimacy with God; we were spiritually dead without hope of ever changing. Our lives, however respectable they appeared on the outside, were masked; masks hid the hurts and damage wrought by our own actions and decisions, and those of others. And some of us lived that way for a long time.

Then, according to God's foreknowledge, we got a revelation. Oh Lord, how enormous and wide ranging is your arsenal of ways to reveal Yourself to us! But we got there—*the Cross was for me!* Salvation and healing and hope were for me, *for me personally*. We said yes, aligned ourselves with the work and victory of the Cross, and passed over from death to life. We passed over. We were transferred.

Now, as a (fairly) fanatical football fan, (can you be

fairly fanatical?) I imagine myself wearing a black football shirt and, following my transfer to a new team, the Kingdom of God, I now wear a white one. I may consider that I have played well or badly today, but *I am wearing the shirt*. I have a right to wear the shirt and to enjoy the privileges of belonging because the transfer fee was settled on my behalf; the badge clearly says "God's Kingdom" on it and despite the muddy terrain of the day or week, it's a white shirt underneath. And though I still remember many of my moves and tactics learned under the previous management, I now belong to a new team.

The shirt is white. The Bible calls it a robe of righteousness (Rev. 6:1). It's the robe that carries the righteousness; it's the robe that signals my new condition. My new contract. My new covenant in Jesus.

You cannot rent one of these robes, and you can't buy it with your own money. It is bought and paid for on your behalf!

Once received and fitted, we need to get used to wearing it. The Holy Spirit wants to reveal the stunning identity that we have now been born into.

I have been transferred and re-clothed, have a new manager, and play (I live) in a new arena. And my team has won before a ball is kicked!

Football commentators often say that players are afraid to really express themselves for the fear of making mistakes and causing their team to lose. Well, the kingdom of God has already won. Darkness has not overcome it. That fixture was settled two thousand years ago at the

Cross and although the game continues into its latter stages, the result is assured. Jesus has (and all those who are in Him have) won the victory (1 Cor. 15:57).

We are new a creation in Jesus; the old has gone and a new has come. Not "will come." If we say it "will come" then we will wait forever experientially because it has already come. If you will excuse the swift change in analogy, there is no point in waiting at a station for a train that has already passed through.

At the same time, as I mentioned earlier, we have learned over many years to play as we did with a black shirt on our backs. There is considerable un-learning to do. There are knots and tangles to untie. There is *un-life* (pardon my English—you wouldn't believe I am an English teacher, would you?) to dispose of.

Some of those knots we picked up from well-meaning believers who were not free of tangles themselves. They tried, and succeeded, to impose their knotted ways on us. And so, knotted we became. This may have taken on various, religious guises.

Perhaps we picked up that God is more accepting of us if we attend a lot of services and meetings. Or that He is especially accepting when we read the Bible or remember to pray for someone. Maybe we came to believe that the Cross has forgiven us our past sins, but not our future ones, resulting in us living a tense, nervous existence, ready to confess each and every misdemeanor for fear of being rejected and excluded from God's presence.

Perhaps we were knotted with the belief that it is

dangerous to experience the power of the Holy Spirit and the presence of God. Or that to do so was prideful, showing off. The enemy is so deceitful.

Perhaps we have begun to work hard in the kingdom. Now, there is nothing wrong with that if we are partnering with the Holy Spirit. His kind of work is not a burden to us. But when we believe that so much depends on us personally and take on a yoke of anxiety, we cannot be living in the freedom of the Cross.

Only the Spirit can birth Spirit. No amount of religiosity or religious effort can do that. Remember when Jesus talked about the fruit from trees?

> For the tree is known by its fruit.
> —MATTHEW 12:33

Perhaps, deep down, we think the Father is angry or disappointed with us. We have come to relate to Jesus as our Lord, and as a friend. We welcome the presence of the Holy Spirit and enjoy Him, but the Father, He is still somewhat distant, stiff, remote, and somehow disapproving.

We would do well to re-read, or remember, the undignified behavior of the father in the parable of the prodigal son (Luke 15). Before a word had left the prodigal's lips, as he returned to his father with a sense of deep shame, the father had left his vantage point where he was looking out for his son, gathered up his tunic, ran out towards his son, and then fell upon his neck.

What would that look like to you, the Father falling upon your neck?

Lord God, show me something of Your passion for me. Touch my heart at its core. Let Your passion for me become part of me, part of my experienced relationship with You. Let love blossom where a sense of duty has previously dominated. Amen.

Perhaps long stretches of your spiritual experience have been dry, dusty, uneventful, boring. You may admit that the immediate sense of God's presence has not been a regular or recent experience.

God is not thrown or at all shocked by our transparency before Him.

Perhaps something happened. Something tragic. Something unfair. One of those *Why would God allow...?* things. Your questions and disappointment, maybe even a sense of shock and dismay, have pushed aside the sense of God's immediate attention to you. We cannot ignore some of these struggles, and God would not want us to do so. He is Light and would have us bring everything that concerns us to Him, the Light of the World.

He is able to reveal Himself, and our place in Him, through tough times. As it says in one of the Psalms, sometimes we feel that we are at our wits' end (Ps. 107:27). A carelessly tossed verse or cliché is not appropriate or welcomed.

There are knots and tangles.

Perhaps you (and *I* have done a lot of this) have tried to sort out a difficult situation, a relationship, a family affair or a struggle at work. And the tangle has gotten worse. Sometimes we are like a little child who brings a tangled mess to his father, a father who assures him that He will deal with it, but the child returns constantly to try to unpick the knots himself, giving the problem his constant attention, whilst the father waits for him to remove his fumbling, little fingers. The child thinks that he needs to *see* the process to be truly reassured; are we not like this? "Is Father really going to deal with this?" we question. "Does He care about it as much as I do?" Sometimes, however, we need to walk away from it and trust Him to resolve matters His way.

It is perhaps only when we have seen the fruit of His abilities that we see in a new way that this dependent attitude is the wiser one. Something of life has been revealed to us. *Wow, Lord, you really want to look after this issue for me and resolve it your way...* Thank you, Lord. I like the Good News Bible translation of Proverbs 3:5:

> Trust in the Lord with all your heart. Never rely on what you think you know.

The Message puts it like this:

> Trust in the Lord from the bottom of your heart; don't try to figure out everything on your own.

OCD and Legalism

Some tangles take a while to make themselves evident. I discovered in 2007 that I was suffering with Obsessive Compulsive Disorder—this is often shortened to OCD.

You may be familiar with (sometimes comical) anecdotes and representations of those who struggle with this. A familiar scenario might be the need to check that a door has been locked time and time again, or straightening all the tins in the cupboard, or washing your hands several times for fear of contamination (or for fear of contaminating others.)

More serious cases involve those wrapped in guilt, confessing to crimes even before they have a remote chance of happening. A man drops a sweet in the street, the sweet rolls into the road, and he simply *must* pick it up; otherwise, a child may see it, run into the road, be hit by a car and *he* would be responsible for the child's death. What may seem a preposterous argument for him being responsible, may be very real to someone who has not had the security of the Father's love embedded in the core of his heart, and has become normalized to this way of thinking through fear.

My OCD was of the religious nature. The official term is "scrupulosity." You see, this had been dormant in me for years, but now God was bringing it out into the light. I had been aware, when I was young, of the temptation to confess to something I might have done wrong. I would touch something—a car perhaps, and then see a scratch and somehow convince myself that I was responsible for it. The process of coming into freedom concerning this disorder was extremely painful, not just for me, but for some dear friends as well. I can praise God for the healing He has brought, but do not underestimate the waves that it caused, too, to those around me. I also learned much about God's grace in this—grace shown me by those close to me was grace beyond grace on occasions; which is, of course, what grace essentially is. God was unearthing some core misgivings I held about Him, some core inner beliefs that were lies. Fear hides in the darkness of lies.

Jesus wants us to live in freedom from addictions and compulsions; His desire is for us to enjoy abundant life (John 10:10). Abundant life shared and spilling over is the most effective form of evangelism on the planet; sons discovering that they can live, stemming from an identity of being much loved royalty!

I saw how I had doubted my salvation, frequently. I saw that I was afraid of God and angry at Him. When I considered the bullying I had taken at school years before, I could hardly contain my fury and sense of bewilderment as I questioned where God had been during this torment. In this phase of my life, with OCD plaguing me at its peak, I was guilt ridden. I would hear myself say something and would then need to apologize in case I had exaggerated or not quite told the truth in every respect. This was pseudo vigilance to the extreme, and at the time, I did not see just how bound I was by legalistic religion and law. I knew I was bound, but I needed revelation.

We are primarily supernatural beings and we need revelation. Revelation from the tree of life. Remember God's initial command to Adam and Eve? They could eat from all the trees in the garden, including the tree of life, but not from the tree of the knowledge of good and evil. I would like to unpack this a little later, but let me say here that God's design was for men to live in dependence upon Him, upon His words of life, His transparent truth, and not upon reasoning, judgment, and limited parameters of understanding.

We need His living, breathed word. Sometimes our thoughts are reasonable (reason-able), but He has something more fitting than our reasoning to say or to show us.

I remember praying with someone, many years ago, for a lady who shared that she was seeing Unidentified Flying Objects (UFOs) from her bedroom window. As she shared I called upon the Holy Spirit—this was weird stuff, and I didn't know how to really respond or how to help her. But God did. He simply showed us that the lady was lonely. We asked the Holy Spirit to comfort her and bring her peace. He knew where the lady was really at; to be honest, I cannot quite remember what became of the UFO element. That was not the issue at heart.

I was absolutely saved by grace, but living in bondage to a "pointing finger" of judgment, an accusing voice that sought to measure me (and constantly declare me wanting) against pure and holy standards. In other words, I was in bondage to legalism, to law. I am sure many of my tears must have been Jesus' as I floundered in guilt.

I really began to despair of getting free. I was totally desperate. I was ill. I would goad myself into doing things I was afraid of because if fear was a sin, then the only way I could prove my obedience was to take on the fear. And of course, this drive to prove my innocence was never quite satisfied. There was always one more thing to do. One more thing to do. One more step to take, one more law to satisfy, but the law was never satisfied.

Law is never satisfied, it never rests. It does not build and encourage but consumes us and debilitates. It always seeks to show you where you have fallen short. The Law, let us remember, was given to reveal to men that they needed a Savior, that they would be unable to keep the Law. Grace always seeks to show us how complete we have become in our new identities in Jesus.

The Holy Spirit is convicting the world of its sin—of its need of a savior—and He is convicting us of our righteousness in Jesus (John 16:8-13).

Really, I was living in denial of the Cross. I couldn't see it, but that is the truth. The entire price for my innocence had already been paid. One of my leaders, praying for me on one occasion, shared that it was as if I was constantly trying to sweep a swept, clean room. All I was doing was kicking up the dust from the broom, confusing the picture. Sweep, sweep, sweep. All of this activity was pointless and hugely exhausting.

I thank God that freedom was coming and that, now, I am (largely) free of OCD. My leaders and the body have supported me considerably. Kind people spent time with me on the telephone. I read articles and began to recognize my wrong thinking against the truth.

How we need the body of Christ. We all have Christ,

but we need His expression in each other as this body of Christ grows from its Head, Jesus.

Others may not have fallen prey to such struggles as I had, there will have been other challenges, but the issue of law and grace is a key, I believe, to many in the body, and key to the body continuing to mature in the Lord and live as royal sons and daughters.

As I write, the United Kingdom has recently witnessed the funeral of Lady Margaret Thatcher, the first (and only, to date) female Prime Minister in the United Kingdom. Her motto was "Cherish Freedom."

Let's talk some more about freedom and legalism. Life and law.

Chapter 7

THIS IS HUGE

*The Law [was] only a shadow of
the good things to come.*

—HEBREWS 10:1

The reality... is found in Christ.

—COLOSSIANS 2:17, NIV

I HAVE AMAZING CHURCH leaders. I imagine that I might survive being a pastor for about twenty-eight minutes, half an hour on a good day. Church leaders clearly have a lot of responsibilities, and at times they must weigh heavily. They want to see their people grow in Jesus, stay in the truth, not get side tracked, or, worse still, shipwrecked.

The wider church needs its pastors to learn that the

way to keep their people on course is to release them—
to release them to the ultimate Shepherd, to hold them
very loosely, to teach them whilst at the same time
allowing them to discover the reality of Jesus for themselves. To control is to bind. Control stunts revelation
of life.

> What then? Shall we sin because we are not
> under law but under grace? May it never be!
>
> —ROMANS 6:15

Paul discusses this, doesn't he? He discusses the con-
sequences of living in the Law and recognizes and con-
fronts the potential accusation that he will be considered
to be lenient on sin. Surely it is better to set rules, guide-
posts and landmarks, to insist on certain behaviors for
our own good and for the good of the Body of Christ?
But I have seen in my life and in the lives of others that
legalism demands a high price and does not produce
"abundant life." How can what man contrives result in
what issues from the Spirit of God?

As one who has known what it is to be ensnared by
religiosity, let me say that discovering that it is the kindness of the Lord that produces real repentance has absolutely changed my outlook.

> The kindness of God leads you to repentance.
>
> —ROMANS 2:4

Oh, how much deeper is the love of Christ than we
imagine! How much more thorough and targeted is His
work in our lives! He is so very personal. His attention

to us is intimate, crafted, and totally purposeful. When we get revelation of how kind He is, we change. He is not loose on sin. He paid the greatest price to deal with sin. If we can grasp this, then, rather than producing license in us, it produces hunger in us for Him because we are all hungry for love at our core. We know what real love is, deep down. We know what looks like love, and we discover what may masquerade as love, but, deep to deep, we recognize the real thing. Paul says that we have an anointing in us (1 John 2:20) and that it remains; that anointing, the Holy Spirit presence in us, counsels us, and He witnesses to us what is real and what is fake.

We don't want the fake, do we? Do we want a form of religion that denies the genuine power of the kingdom? (2 Tim. 3:5). We thirst for the pure, refreshing water of life.

Life speaks. Life flows. Life echoes with our spirit man. Life releases. Life unties. Jesus is life, and He gives us permission to live freely as His children, allowing the Father to father us. Even though our Father may discipline us from time to time, His heart is to liberate us from the fake, into the real, regal reality.

As God has been revealing his love to me, my appetites have been changing. At times the first step has been for Him to show me what is underneath a particular appetite or sin in my life. Yes, He cares enough to counsel us and teach us, as a good Father.

Joseph Prince (in his book *Destined to Reign* published by Harrison House) describes how a member of his congregation who was struggling to give up smoking expressed her frustration to him. She tried and tried but could not seem to stop. Every new resolution failed.

Of course, resolutions (at New Year or at any other time) are very likely to fail. They may result in a change of behavior for a season, but are unlikely to be ultimately successful. Only an internal shift can do that, and only the Holy Spirit knows how to bring that about.

Pastor Prince reassured his church member and encouraged her to stand strong on who she is in Jesus. She is the righteousness of Christ! So are we! Jesus has settled that. When she wanted to smoke, she would continue to stand on her identity in Jesus. Sometimes she smoked and sometimes she didn't, but she refused to set up a law (a resolution) that could only focus her on her behavior and (as Paul teaches) empower her to fail. She focused squarely on her identity. She was turning to Life in her addiction and battling in the Spirit; when her body screamed for nicotine, rather than focus on how she was about to perform (make a judgment against herself), she focused on who she is in Jesus, the life-giver.

One day she woke up and went about her day, and realized that she no longer wanted to smoke. She was free. Not because she had been told not to smoke, not because she had beaten herself up about it, not because she had received condemnation, but because the reality, the power and the life within her had risen to a degree to which she no longer desired the tobacco. The kindness of God had led her to repentance. Life had overcome an area of death in her experience.

I am seeking to follow a similar approach in my own struggles. It is so liberating to realize that I am accepted by my heavenly Father, that I belong to Him, that the Alpha and Omega is working on my behalf and is, step by step, transforming me to make me more like Jesus. Actually, to make me increasingly the real Steve who will reflect the life of Jesus as only Steve can! This is a move from legality to regality.

When I fail, I assert who I am in Jesus, the righteousness of Christ, and, as Pastor Prince pictures, I continue on, thanking Him for His precious blood which washes me as I walk. Yes, I walk under a moving fountain of cleansing grace, and so do you.

This is a gospel of good news. Mentioning evangelism previously, I would emphasize that witnessing to those around us is not going to be difficult as we live from this wonderful place where He has seated us; in heavenly places with Jesus. Witnessing is hard work when it all has to be explained, especially when the external evidence is thin on the ground! When the life is seen, evangelism (sharing Him and who we have become in Him) seems to flow very naturally. We are partnering with the Holy Spirit. The Holy Spirit loves people!

Because it isn't really about us, at the end of the day, is it? It isn't a personal, earthly, temporary kingdom that we are trying to build. Life is about Jesus and the expression of Him from heaven, here on earth.

Chapter 8

TO BE LIKE JESUS

*And they were all amazed at the
greatness of God... everyone was
marveling at all that He was doing.*

—LUKE 9:43

JESUS ATTRACTED PEOPLE. He attracted them for
good and, sometimes, as opposition. The needy and
broken were drawn to Him because they saw power,
love, ability and hope in His nature. People saw that He
was very different from religious authority figures, those
who, Jesus said, imposed burdens on people without
lifting a finger to help them. Religion and legalism are
hard taskmasters. To the degree to which we are held
in the grip of legalism, we will, by God's grace, discover
that to be the case.

Those with hard hearts were drawn to Him because they could not understand how someone who lived from an opposite spirit to theirs could wield so much influence. These people had to work very hard to keep their influence, to maintain their positions. Jesus was simply, intrinsically influential. The religious authorities had to spin their plates or they and their plates would fall. Jesus had no need to do so—His momentum was from a different spirit, a different kingdom.

It's a good reminder for us, too. Seeking influence might well be hard work for us. Living His life, however, may bring us influence in some very unexpected quarters.

Sometimes in the kingdom you may be thrust into the limelight. If this happens, and you wonder if you can cope with it, if you should be there, if you know that only God and His enabling can sustain you there, you are probably in the right place. Those who wish to be in the limelight may react negatively when they are positioned out of it. In or out, the Lord is interested in building His kingdom and He will place us where we are going to be the most effective.

It will be interesting in eternity to meet the millions of amazing people who we have never heard of, who perhaps achieved more significant accomplishments than many that we have! And let's remember, significant doesn't necessarily mean grand or huge. Kingdom impact can be very unassuming at times in natural terms. More than once, Jesus did miracles and actually told those touched by Him *not* to go spread the news.

He knew what would contribute most effectively to His kingdom agenda.

You may speak compassionately to someone tomorrow who, touched by His life in you, goes on to change a nation. Do we really care who gets the credit? Hopefully, we care that Jesus gets the credit; the anointing to change lives is His and He does all things well.

It has been said that Jesus never appeared to run anywhere, to rush; He had no fretful timetable to keep pace with. He always had quality time for those he was with and ministered to, and was never late. Jesus Himself gives us the key to this when He says that He only did, and does, what He sees His Father doing (John 5:19).

Lord, let the same be said of us. May we live simple lives, keeping in step with You.

We fill our days with so much activity; much of it can be church activity too. I believe the scripture that says He has given us a light burden, not a heavy yoke (Matt. 11:30). If we are under constant pressure and stress, we need to pause and take a look, with Jesus, at what is going on. I am not talking about the kind of pressures which some of our overseas family in Christ may suffer due to harsh regimes and other forms of discrimination. Some of those stresses are more understandable, and the Lord promises grace for those too. Some of our stresses may originate in that we are strenuously active outside His enabling.

We sometimes have our own agendas even in the midst of the body ministry. As we lay these down and step into His rest, He strips us of unnecessary busyness. We see that we have enough time for what He has called us to do, or, more accurately, for *whom* He has called us to *be*. We partner with Him, we partner in what we see He is doing. At times this may be a lot less, or it may be more, than we assume. My experience is that it is usually less, but my involvement is more effective for playing the right part—and much less tiring!

REST

Hebrews 4:9 tells us there remains the Sabbath rest for the people of God. We live in much changed times. When I was a lad, most shops were closed on Sundays! I would feel guilty for even buying a newspaper!

As the years have gone by, times have certainly changed. I am not saying here whether for the better or for the worse. But today, most shops are open on Sundays here in the UK, sports fixtures are regularly played too, and for many working people, Sunday is as any other day of the week. Sunday may be a family's only opportunity for time together, and it embraces as much busyness as a working day.

Some churches have embraced this realization very practically by recognizing how much modern lifestyles have changed. Christian services are held on a different day of the week, perhaps on a Friday or Saturday night, since that is when most people tend to go out.

The day of rest is no longer what it was. But here is the good news! In Jesus, it was never meant to be a single day of the week! That rest was always meant to be a daily experience for the believer! We live in rest because we are in Christ now. We are empowered to live His life—He lives in and through us—hence, toil is no longer our portion. We might have to work hard, and often so, but there is a settled rest in Jesus that says "all is well, I am provided for, I am looked after." I work not to survive; I am working because in the Cross I have already survived and better than that, I am moving from provision to provision; the boundary lines have fallen, for me, in pleasant places (Ps. 16). I am not under pressure because pressure is an acceptance of fear, and I am not going to fear in Jesus. If He is for me, who or what can be against me?

We will enjoy our holidays much more if we begin them from a place of rest!

THIS LIFE

This life is a heavenly life, and I have to admit I feel like a novice. The Bible is true; it is the Word of God that reveals the living Word of God, who is Jesus. Many of us have come to faith through believing what the Scripture says about us and about what Jesus has accomplished for us. Will we believe only some of it or all of it? Is one part of the Bible any less the Word of God than another?

Do you believe that you are seated in heavenly places with Jesus Christ? Well, technically, yes. Theoretically, yes. Theologically, yes. If we stop there we are going to deny ourselves so much of the life that Jesus wants to live through us and bless us with. Maybe you believe that when you die you will go to heaven. The Bible says that you are never going to die, so how does that work? If you are never going to die, then this new eternal life He has given you must have started already. You now live from heaven, on earth. Heaven is within you; heaven's spirit (the Holy Spirit) lives within you. God wants to open our eyes to the reality of this heaven in which we have been placed (You are seated in heavenly places) and to the reality of the spiritual happenings going on around us. Kingdom life is a regal life.

You are well known in the heavenly realm. You are marked out. I believe your seal is visible. You can access heavenly resources right now: healing, wisdom, and help. Heaven's angels are on call—did you know that? They take great joy in supporting us and helping us. The Bible describes them as ministering spirits (Heb. 1:14). In Jesus you have the authority to acquire angelic help in difficult circumstances or to send angels to others who are in need.

This is not a book about angels in particular, but let me give you an example. This happened to a friend of mine who was driving home in the evening along a dual carriageway (a highway with two lanes). There were two lanes in both directions. She was behind a car and decided to pass it, so she began to pull across to the other lane. Right at that moment, a voice from the back of her car said sternly, "Don't!"

Seconds later a car flashed past her with no lights on, coming in the opposite direction on the wrong side of the central reservation. Praise God, her life and that of the other drivers, were quite possibly saved from destruction. Angels are real. They are as real as anything we have experienced in our Christian lives.

I have had limited experience of angels, myself. Now is not the place to describe those encounters I have had, but I appreciate and value the attention and ministry that angels give us.

We are supernatural people. Our spirit has been made alive. Our body carries our spirit and our soul (our soul is who we really are in our thinking and our hearts). I believe we have a wonderful opportunity to look within to the kingdom that resides within us and to be expectant of what God is doing among us. He is no respecter of persons, is He? From the youngest to the oldest, boys and girls, men and women, He loves to express Himself to us and through us, and all this knowing that, at the end of our course on earth, we are going to be with Him, face to face, forever.

> *Oh, Lord, please give us Your heavenly perspective. You want to reveal Yourself to us, but also want to reveal the real "us" to us.*

We know that the whole creation is groaning and longing to see what real church is!

This life is entirely because of the Cross.

Chapter 9

THE CROSS

*For you have died and your life is
hidden with Christ in God.*

—COLOSSIANS 3:3

P AUL ENCOURAGES US to grow up in Him, not
laying again the foundations and basic teachings
of our faith. But let's not misunderstand this. He
also says there is no foundation other than which has
already been laid (1 Cor. 3:11). In short, we can never
move away from the central significance of the Cross
of Jesus.

I remember hearing a testimony that I thought was
tragic. A young woman said she had given up her
Christianity to turn to Islam because every time she

looked at the Cross, she felt guilty. Islam, she added, gave her a simpler set of guidelines to follow.

The opposite should have been true! The flesh would rather turn to a religion than a relationship of life because there is more control and predictability in a same-old, same-old religion. The flesh wants rules.

The Cross does not cry out, "You are guilty!" It cries out, "You are innocent; your guilt was nailed here forever! That old sinful man in you died with Me. Throw off that old skin and walk out of it!" Praise God for the Cross and the precious blood of Jesus—that pure untainted blood (unlike ours) which was shed to buy us back, and, moreover, to empower us to live a new life— His resurrected life. That life stems from the Cross. That life is in the Cross and the risen life provided to us is formed in us. The Cross will never be old-hat. It is central to everything.

Of course, it must have been a somber meal that Jesus shared with His disciples in some respects. They found out that one of them was going to betray Jesus. But remember that Jesus told them how much He had been looking forward to the meal together. John was leaning on Jesus; it seems it was quite a relaxed time together. I have enjoyed celebrating communion (as we call it) in many different ways; some have been more serious and others quite relaxed as we have shared bread and juice and enjoyed this meal together.

Such meals in Jesus' day and prior to His time on earth were a genuine invitation to intimacy and acceptance. Frequently, we see in Scripture that visitors were offered a meal as part of their welcome to someone's house. Do you remember that when the angels arrived at Abraham's tent, the first thing he did was to offer them food (Gen. 18)?

We want to fully appreciate (which we can only do by revelation of the Holy Spirit) the depths of what Jesus did at the Cross without any false religiosity. It is an awesome thing to personally come to the Cross and reckon (as Paul puts it) that you died there with Jesus, and that you are now risen with Him. Let's remember that we can live this Holy Spirit life now because we are risen with Him, seated in heavenly places far above all rule and authority.

> *Lord, we died with You on the Cross and are risen with You; we are seated in heavenly places with You. Touch our hearts and minds that we would expect to be increasingly aware of the reality of where we are. We are in heaven, now, and heaven is in us and will touch this earthly domain in which we temporarily reside. Let Your presence be known around us!*

Yes, we can pray with confidence because we have the authority of His name. We are His ambassadors. We are endowed with His authority; we carry and represent Him. As we sense the confidence of the Holy Spirit to pray, we can make requests of Him boldly and increasingly *declare* and *decree* upon the basis of the finished work of the Cross.

We do not need to settle for "If it be your will" prayers.

The Word shows us much of His will, and where we do not clearly know His will, we can pray in the Holy Spirit (in tongues) and also declare the kingdom of God and His order in situations. It is not pride to pray with authority. The enemy will try to accuse you saying, "Who do you think you are? Look what you did yesterday!" We are sons and daughters in the kingdom. A good day or a bad day does not alter that.

Sometimes I don't know what is right to pray in this or that situation. Especially if I have a vested interest, I need to take care not to try and pray in a controlling fashion—this is unwise at best and dangerous at worst. I will pray in the Holy Spirit and on occasions will begin to have a sense of the right way to pray. If not, I can pray, "Lord I speak divine order into this situation—glorify Yourself; let kingdom order reign in this." I am always confident to pray in this way because it agrees with the Word of God. Be careful of praying, "Let so and so do this or that." In this way we are often trying to work things out our way, to exercise our own control, but we don't want our way, we want His!

The Cross and following resurrection of Jesus are the most powerful events in history. And you are part of them! You are evidence that the word of God has always been the truth. The Bible says that there will be no end to the kingdom of God, and here you and I are, carrying His life in the twenty-first century! That's exciting.

Chapter 10

LIFE—THE TWO TREES

*God did create a world without
sin. We just screwed it up.*

—WESLEY MILLER[1]

O FTEN SAID IN jest, you are about to utter some
discerning words. They have become a well-
known phrase. Someone begins to share a
funny story with you; perhaps something embarrassing
or distasteful that happened to them. As the amount of
detail grows, you decide that you have heard enough:

"Too much information!" you answer back, hoping
that you are spared any further comment!

The events in the Garden of Eden are legendary. I
would like to focus on one particular aspect. Why was

it so dangerous for Adam and Eve to eat from the tree of the knowledge of good and evil?

Adam and Eve had lived perfectly with the Father in the garden. They lived from a place of dependence upon Him. They did not learn anything in Eden that they did not need to know. Father provided all that they needed. There was no conflict, no arguments, no fruitless reasoning and no confusion. They knew that God knew everything, and they were satisfied and at peace with that. The enemy's promise that there was more to be had by knowing was a lie. Adam and Eve were not designed for that kind of responsibility. Their part was to live in relationship with the Father. That's the regal life.

Having yielded to Satan's trap, a new dimension to life was born. Knowing needlessly, resulting in making judgments, and because they had entered the realm of disobedience, shame was now active in their experience for the first time. They wanted to hide. They felt exposed. The nakedness they now knew was not primarily a physical one. It was about a loss of identity. Vulnerability and uncovering had now entered their psyche. This was a mighty fall from their previous standing of divine order and right relationship. And in place of dependence upon the Father, a self-willing reasoning and desire for knowledge had been birthed.

All of us were born in this condition! We were born with a sinful need to make our own way—to reason, to see, and to decide what was and wasn't right. No wonder for some it can be a crushing responsibility to live in this way! It reminds me of the people of Israel who had to make bricks for the Egyptians; at one stage in Pharaoh's anger they had to collect their own straw too and still maintain the quota of bricks. Sometimes we have felt that we were trying to build and yet lacked the wisdom to do it; we would scrap around searching for clues.

Christ has restored us to our former position. In Jesus, the source of life, we once again can eat from revealed truth, from the tree of life. No longer do we have to rely on our own reasoning. No longer do we need to fearfully try and see around the corner to see what is coming, or pontificate endlessly on how a situation may or may not work itself out. Jesus frees us from the never ending "I should…" and "I should have…" and releases us to move on with the peace and life of the Holy Spirit who lives in us.

Before encountering the Spirit life, many of us have been used to reasoning our way through life's decisions and difficulties. We may have been aware of God's Word and guidance from time to time, but on the whole, we have endeavored to work out our way forward more often than not.

There is a better way for us, an easier way, in the sense that there is a place of rest, His rest, where we can adopt a different perspective.

He loves to take responsibility for us. He wants us to give Him the space to speak to us. He wants us to remain in peace. There will be times (as has happened in my experience) where He leaves a choice to us. "What would you like to do? What is on your heart?" He says to us. It may be a narrow way into the kingdom, but once in it, there are times when He gives us a lot of liberty with our decision making as we walk our lives in the comfort of the Holy Spirit and the Word.

It is especially a blessing to walk in His revelation during life's storms. I have experienced times when my life was so tossed about, and when I was so terribly anxious, I was desperate to act in a situation and bring some stability. The more I meddled, the more confused I became.

I needed to learn—and I think over the years I have learned to an extent—to pause, to wait, to not fret, and to allow Holy Spirit to go before me and steady the boat. At times, the right thing for me to do was nothing. At other times, once brought into a degree of rest, I was then able to take firm, unhurried steps which would contribute to a situation's resolution. The tree of life is good fruit; it feeds, it nourishes, it strengthens—it benefits us. Eating of it, we remember that we are dependent upon Jesus and not on ourselves, the way it was always designed to be.

Royal sons and daughters are to live in peace, in divine rest.

Chapter 11

THE SUPERNATURAL

*The Spirit of the Lord snatched Philip
away... Philip found himself at Azotus.*

—ACTS 8:39–40

HAVING BAPTIZED AN Ethiopian, Philip disappears.

Excuse me?

He disappeared and then became aware that he was in a different location. If we thought that the science fiction world such as that of *Star Trek* was ahead of us in its fantasy, it's time to think again.

Many of us grew up with a sense that we need to be afraid of what we do not understand. Hollywood has played its part in that! "Be afraid, be very afraid!" If it's out there, and you don't understand it, it's hostile, stronger than you, and it's out to get you!

Perhaps, like I did, you tinkered with spiritual interests before coming to know Jesus. I thank God that I did not do much more than tinker. Some reading this will have lived lives with a great deal of involvement in the occult and alternative spiritual paths.

There is a whole raft of them. You can easily obtain some excellent reference materials which describe their beliefs and practices. But you will find that all of them have their roots outside Christ, and that is not the kingdom we are a part of in Jesus.

I thank God because I see that He kept me from a deeper involvement than I might have had. Thank you, Lord, for your grace. I tinkered with astrology—the belief that precisely 8.3 percent, or one person in every twelve, of the world's population is going to have a similar experience every day—but not much more than that.

I enjoy the supernatural! We were made that way! We were designed to want to explore, to discover, to experience wonders, to be amazed, and to make personal discoveries. The Bible says that God has set eternity in the hearts of men (Eccles. 3:11). Eternity—wow—oh, that the Holy Spirit would unveil more of the reality of this to us!

We know that Satan, masquerading as an angel of light, offers a plethora of promises of discovery and enlightenment, but we know too that his only intention is to keep people bound in error and away from Jesus, the Light of the World and the light of life. The Bible says that God is light, and that there is no darkness in Him at all (1 John 1:5).

God's desire is to reveal! His ways are beyond our natural thinking, but He has now made us alive in Christ, with the mind of Christ. It is a walk of faith (and not sight), but at the same time His heart is to share with those He is intimate with.

It's interesting that the last book of the Bible is called Revelation, not Secrecy! Imagine that, "Please, all, turn to the book of Secrecy." There would be one chapter and one verse: "'I have nothing to share with you,' says the Lord. Amen." What a disappointment.

But if you and I are in Jesus, we have a lot to look forward to in the Holy Spirit and nothing to fear from the supernatural realm. I remember when I was first saved at university, a few of us seemed to have a curiously negative interest in those we knew were, or believed were, involved with the occult. These people were dangerous! They were the enemy!

People are not our enemy! Of course, we need to be wise around those who may not have our best interests at heart. But our real enemy has his hands on people, and their shackles to the occult can be overcome by Jesus' love just as our own variety of shackles have been, and are being, broken.

We have nothing to fear, but fear can prevent us from enjoying the supernatural ride that our Father has for us! Joel prophesied that we would dream and see visions. There is nothing weird about this. It is our birthright to live from our supernatural position in heavenly places as royal sons and daughters.

Your first step into the kingdom was a supernatural event! Why should any of the following steps be any different?

God wants us to be alive to the amazing supernatural environment in which we live. We may not be aware of it, or we may just occasionally brush shoulders with it, but it is there nonetheless, and it is where exploits are taking place.

A PANORAMA

His life includes dreams and visions, divine appointments, divine re-scheduling, holy moments when you are praying in a church meeting or alone at home, waking up with a particular song going around your head, waking up in the middle of the night and sensing a gentle peace in the room, and waking up and having a surprising desire to pray for someone or to pray into a particular situation.

His life includes knowing a particular need that someone has before they tell you and thinking of a particular scripture for someone who needs it. It includes deciding (to your own surprise) to visit a different coffee shop to the one you usually go to, where you happen to run into an old friend that you haven't seen in a long time, who then shares a difficult circumstance with you that you are able to pray into with them. "Fancy seeing you in here, today…" but it was no accident.

And after a hard day, when you have burnt the dinner,

shouted at your spouse, been overly harsh with your noisy children, deliberately ignored the inner, gentle prompting to try out that new coffee shop, lost your temper with someone at church because they criticized your choice of subject for the Bible study—after all of that, His supernatural life in you enables you to rest your head on His chest, receive His affirmation and love, knowing that you are a precious child of His, and that you are permanently the righteousness of Christ (2 Cor. 5:21). "I love you—let's go again tomorrow!" He whispers to you.

WACKY EXPERIENCES

"I heard so and so on the Christian channel say that they went to heaven." "Julia saw three angels in the service this morning—two blue ones and a purple one!" "Apparently Melissa's cancer has—well—gone." "You wouldn't believe it, but four people in our church had the same verse on their hearts when they woke up this morning." "Some of my friends make *ho*-ing noises when they pray and when they worship." "Usually when we worship, I get tired of the same song after three or four times, but this morning we stayed on the same song for forty minutes and God's presence was powerful!"

Yesterday, as I write, a friend of mine told me that her friend's leg had grown *in front of her eyes* whilst receiving prayer. If "nothing is impossible with God," why might we doubt occurrences such as this?

I suppose it is only wacky if I have not experienced

it, if it is outside my normal parameters. None of us are alone in this.

Wacky things happened in the Bible too. Jesus spat on someone and they got their sight back (Mark 8:23). A whole people group walked through a sea because God caused the waters to gather up on each side (Exod. 14). A nation had an instant plague of frogs and of locusts and their water was turned to blood (Exod. 8). That's wacky.

Someone listening to the apostle Paul died after falling from a third floor window. Paul prayed for him and he came back to life (Acts 20:9). An army marched around a city in silence for a while and after marching around it for a final time, with a shout, the walls of the city collapsed (Josh. 6). Mm, that's an interesting approach to military strategy, don't you think? A man who used to extort money from the poor met Jesus and then, after a meal with Him (remember the significance of intimacy and a meal?) apologized and restored what he had extorted four times over (Luke 19). That's wacky; that's supernatural. On one occasion, Peter was in prison and the church was praying for his release (Acts 12). God answered, and an angel led him out of prison as the guards failed to see him. When Peter knocked on the door where the church was gathered, they did not believe it was him! I just love the transparency of the Bible! I wonder what they were expecting as they prayed—clearly they were not expecting the answer that they received! Imagine the scene:

Believer: "Lord, please release Peter, your servant! Nothing is too difficult for You!"

Everyone: "Amen!"

There is a knock at the door.

Girl, returning from the front door: "Peter is at the door!"

Everyone: "Don't be ridiculous; now where were we? Lord, please release Peter!"

The Old and New Testaments are packed with the supernatural.

Daniel had amazing dreams and visions in the Old Testament and John had them in the New Testament.

The disciples were especially remarkable to the Jewish authorities as they had not been schooled as had they. How could these men be so sure of what they were testifying to? How could they heal the sick? How could they speak so boldly of Jesus the Nazarene when they were so ordinary and did not hold respected positions?

We are in good company. And so often we feel weak and unable because the Bible says God wants to show the world that the power is from Him and not our own. It makes sense, really. If it were ours, we would be responsible for sharing our own righteousness. As it is His, it is His righteousness, and it is available to whosoever will come, wherever they are. He is the source of this life.

Many in today's church are testifying of a fresh experience of God's love and power. He loves to express Himself through His children—of all ages! It's all supernatural, actually. You cannot be born again without a supernatural event having taken place. God has made His home in us.

Lord, I am sorry where I have judged the experiences of others. I acknowledge that I am a supernatural son, and that I have nothing to fear in You. There is no fear in Your kingdom. Please move supernaturally in my life too; I want to dream, see, and hear supernaturally. I want to walk in the comfort of Your Holy Spirit each day. Amen.

Think on this. Jesus said that John the Baptist was the greatest man of God on earth, and that the least in the kingdom of heaven was greater than him (Matt. 11:11). How is your self-image now?

Chapter 12

SPIRITUAL MATURITY

Now to Him who is able to do far more
abundantly beyond all that we ask or think,
according to the power that works within us.

—Ephesians 3:20

G OD'S DESIRE IS, as the verse above suggests, that
we all grow up into our royal sonship. He is the
head of the body of Christ. We are royal sons
of the King of kings. We have been chosen to live in
Him, to live in the vibrant power of the Holy Spirit. We
live in testing, but amazing days when the Spirit of God
is moving across our planet, lighting fires, networking
believers together across boundaries, across denomi-
nations and across nations. We had better get ready to
work closely with brothers and sisters that we had not,

perhaps, considered! The Holy Spirit forges the only true unity and the only genuine, spiritual relationships.

It's a time of blossoming relationships in the Holy Spirit. Our fellowship together in the body of Christ is in the Spirit. It is a life relationship. Gone are the days when we assumed that a church of this or that denomination was necessarily on fire or traditional. God is knocking on the doors and enters where He is welcomed. He doesn't worry about whether your church group has *Free* or *River* or any other specific word or phrase in the title. Is He moving among His people? He wants to inhabit His people. Inhabiting is a much deeper experience than merely visiting, isn't it? You are welcome when you visit someone or somewhere, but you never get too comfortable because you know you will have to leave again. Inhabiting is about staying, resting, being at home, expressing yourself.

> *Lord, express Yourself among us! At home, in church fellowship, in our work places, in our schools and colleges, in the shopping centers, when we are at work, rest, and play!*

As the Lord of lords and King of kings, we invite Him to go further than that—we invite Him to exercise His reign and kingship.

As the Bible says, we learn to cease from our own works. This speaks of rest, of partnering with Jesus, of simply doing what we see Him doing. It speaks of an economy of effort and resources, of a light yoke and an unburdened mandate. We are not trying to build the kingdom as only His Spirit can construct, maintain, and advance it.

The kingdom is being built! He is doing that. The kingdom is advancing. He is seeing to that. Our part is to partner, to co-operate, and to accept His daily invitation to be a part of what He is doing. He said that our part would be to enjoy abundant life. He said that we would not thirst again (John 4:13). Having found Him and His life, we would be satisfied. If we are dissatisfied, let us come swiftly to the Lord of life and the Lord of living, refreshing waters. Seated in heavenly places, we can drink from Him. He wants us to drink, drink, and drink living water!

The woman at the well (John 4) had an encounter with Jesus. Did you notice that she says, "Come, see a man who told me all the things I have done." I don't know how long their conversation was, but such was Jesus' impact on her that she knew she had met someone who knew her inside out. This was the real intimacy she had been looking for. This life in Him is now ours. Let's invite Jesus to reveal more and more of what we have received, to us.

We will expect to see the supernatural operating in our lives, because He is supernatural and lives in us. A supernatural walk will be our norm. Royal sons eat of the kingdom, grow in the kingdom, and grow in authority in the kingdom. They grow and begin to cause the saying "like Father like son" to ring true.

We will refuse to fall into a false humility, asserting that "this isn't for me. I'm not spiritual enough." Frankly, this is nonsense and simply provides an unwelcome opt out. I am going to expect the unexpected. He has my days and my nights. Bring it on, Lord! Thank You for placing me in You, for placing me in Your life. Thank You for paying for all of it. I gladly receive it!

Chapter 13

FINAL THOUGHTS

G IVING CONSIDERATION TO the title of this book, I remembered the television series that used to run throughout the 1970s and 1980s. The show host would surprise an unsuspecting personality and present them with a large red book entitled *This is Your Life*. The individual would then be taken to a TV studio where a resume of his life would take place, interspersed with appearances from past friends and acquaintances. The last guest on the show would usually be the most significant in terms of the chosen individual's life.

Of course, this entire process was retrospective. In our case, God knows all that you have already lived through and also every day that is yet to come. The fact that He knows them all does not mean that you will not have significant choices to make in the future. He does not remove our free will at all, despite knowing the end from the beginning. He's very clever like that.

So, wherever we find ourselves just now, we are in an empowered position to reject legalism in our lives as it is revealed to us, and to embrace a regal identity that is now ours in Jesus Christ.

On some occasions we will have a clear sense of direction from Him, on others less so. You will probably find that He will change the way in which He leads you from time to time. But you will know He leads you and can be confident in that because He has promised to do so.

"Every day is written in your book before one of them came to be," the Bible says in Psalm 139. Amen. And yet in our experience we do not see the end from the beginning in most respects, as God does. Certainly, we know our final end, although much of what surrounds that and what it will look like, we do not know. It certainly will be glorious, free of pain and regret and we will be in perfect health—forever!

For now, what is our attitude going to be?

God's heart is for you and me to know His generous love, to be overwhelmed by it, such that He overflows from us and touches those around us, wherever we are, as I shared earlier.

He does love church meetings, but only those that allow Him to be free. He doesn't enjoy being told to sit still and just watch. Actually, would any of us enjoy that? Mm, I thought not.

He longs to express Himself to us and through us. He loves doing so, and it isn't a hard thing. If we would accept that we can't make kingdom happen (we know that) but are willing to give Him space, He will do so. He will express Himself uniquely through each of us, and as He does, it will all fit together to be a wonderful expression of Him, in His church.

Postscript

ARE YOU HD READY?

As I write, the specification description on TV sets, HD Ready, is already almost superseded by Full HD.

I imagine most of you are more *au fait* with the benefits and advantages of these improved TV models than I am. I mean, I get it; HD (High Definition) is a good thing, and (as I have witnessed on my parents' recent purchase) the added quality is noticeable.

This phrase came to mind as I was walking around my locality just recently, and it came as a question:

"Are you HD ready?"

I like the idea of referring to an intimate walk with Jesus as being high definition. Although we see and know in part (1 Cor. 13) our wonderful Holy Spirit brings revelation to us as kingdom sons, and although it is true that the prophetic operates to different degrees through all of us, there are times when we see more clearly than at others. There are also those brothers and sisters among us who see with greater clarity and precision than we do.

It may be, however, that this book has found its way into the hands of someone whose passion for Jesus and His kingdom has cooled; indeed, maybe you have never personally met Him at all, but your heart is stirred, and you would happily trade your current experience (or lack of it) of God for something fresh, new and vital.

Are you Heaven Destination ready?

You and I can be. We can live from a place where we are ready, in a moment, in the twinkling of an eye, to move from our present, temporary stay here on earth to a permanent kingdom destination.

If we already have a relationship with Jesus, regardless of its potency, the fact is that we are already seated in heavenly places. Our earthly death, whenever that may occur, will merely see us transferred from one domain to another. Our physical body, having ceased to function, will mean that we can no longer live on this earth, and our spirit man will continue to live in heaven. And it will be clothed in a new heavenly body, which will not be overweight, aching, painful, non-functioning or tired!

Nevertheless, the Lord would have us live right now from those heavenly places; this will maximize our wondrous experience of Him on earth and also, as a springtime fragrance, spread kingdom influence around us.

I have a thing about scents. Smells: barbecue, petrol, a newly surfaced road, scents in a forest or garden, fresh coffee. I confess to taking delight in different perfumes (or shall we say *eau de toilette*) from a gent's point of view. I have quite a few. Scents are evocative, rich, invigorating, and powerful. They change the immediate atmosphere around you, and that's exactly what the Holy Spirit wants to do where we are.

For those reading who have never invited Jesus to "take them on" in this life, and who, like the famous woman at the well (John 4), may perhaps be tired of trying to make it in this life under their own steam, please consider this opportunity to take part in an exchange—a divine exchange.

DIVINE EXCHANGE

Become heaven ready. Cross over the bridge to the kingdom of God. Don't be tempted to go all holy: to pray something clever or to change your clothes or hairstyle. If you recognize that you are not living His life and would like to, here is a chance for you.

You and I were born separated from God. Jesus bridged that separation by taking the penalty for your and my condition (and our subsequent actions) on the Cross. He paid that debt. He paid your debt whether you recognized it or not, but you need to redeem your coupon to partner in what He did.

It would be a sad waste if the coupon with your name on it remained unused or unredeemed.

If this resonates with you, I would like to invite

you to simply and genuinely pray the following prayer with me. It may seem a small step for you, but believe me, the step that God is taking toward you is enormous, and you are going to wonderfully discover, life changing.

> *Lord Jesus I believe that You died on the cross and shed Your blood to settle the penalty of my separation from You. Please forgive me for all that I have done wrong, deliberately or otherwise. Likewise, I am ready to forgive any and all who have hurt me. As you freely forgive me, I, equally, release others.*
>
> *I gratefully receive your forgiveness.*
>
> *Please come into my life as my Lord and Savior. Holy Spirit, come into my life and "take me on."*
>
> *You promised to make me new. Yes, Lord, come in and do so and reveal more and more of Yourself to me through the Bible, through other Christians, and through Your Holy Spirit.*
>
> *Thank You, Lord Jesus. Amen.*

Congratulations if you have prayed this and meant it! God has kept His side and done something supernatural in your life.

If you found it difficult to sincerely forgive someone, just bring that to Him. As you are willing, He will work in your life and help you to release those who have meant you harm. He knows everything about you (Ps.

139) and knows how to get through to you. We need to understand that forgiveness matters. Proverbs 18:19 says:

> A brother offended is harder to be won than a
> strong city, and contentions are like the bars of
> a citadel.

We suffer when we do not forgive. We might think that we are holding power over the one who has offended us, but the reality is that the offence is holding us captive.

> He who gets wisdom loves his own soul; he who
> keeps understanding will find good.
> —PROVERBS 19:8

> A man's discretion makes him slow to anger,
> and it is his glory to overlook a transgression.
> —PROVERBS 19:11

You and I are on a journey of discovering His miracle working power in many aspects of life. But the greatest miracle is that He, upon our confession and acceptance of Him, has transferred us from one kingdom to His kingdom.

You are heaven destination ready. How wonderful!

Just as hot coals need other hot coals around them to maintain their temperature; I would encourage you to seek out a friendly, Bible believing church where the Holy Spirit is welcome to express Himself. God will help you to find a place where you can feel at home and grow in your faith. God's Spirit within you is able to work in your life and bring transformation. You will not be able to do this in your own strength, nor are you designed to attempt to do so.

May I wish you every blessing in your walk with Jesus Christ, your friend, Lord and Savior, the King of kings and Lord of lords!

REVELATION LIFE

*A song for the New Zion Christian Fellowship
Conference 2012 "Revelation Life"*

King Jesus now enthroned
Exalted over all
Receive our grateful praise!
Lord, Saviour, Master, Friend
our Source in every need
Your presence is our home

*Open up my ears to hear Your heart
Open up eyes see this Kingdom Life!
Revelation's mine in Christ
Supernatural is my life
Kingdom realm our royal household
Lord my mind I will renew
Tree of Life I eat from You
living always as a royal son in Revelation Life.*

Messiah Lord of grace
Your blood has ransomed me
adopted me as Yours.
My rags are washed away
in scarlet white I stand
a son by Your command!

*Open up my ears to hear Your heart
Open up eyes see this Kingdom Life!
Revelation's mine in Christ
Supernatural is my life
Kingdom realm our royal household
Lord my mind I will renew
Tree of Life I eat from You
living always as a royal son in Revelation Life.*

NOTES

CHAPTER 10: LIFE—THE NEW TREES

1. See http://www.goodreads.com/quotes/tag/adam-and
-eve (accessed September 24, 2013).

ABOUT THE AUTHOR

STEVE HAWKINS TEACHES English as a Second Language in London, and is part of New Zion Christian Fellowship in Welwyn Garden City. After becoming a Christian, Steve came to realize that aspects of legalism were preventing him from enjoying an abundant experience of Holy Spirit life. He was liberated by the Holy Spirit starting with a visit to Toronto Airport Christian Fellowship. He ministers today by leading worship, preaching, and exercising his prophetic gift.

CONTACT THE AUTHOR

steve.hawkins@cheerful.com